snapshot·picture·library

TRAINS

snapshot·picture·library

TRAINS

FOG CITY PRESS

Published by Fog City Press,
a division of Weldon Owen Inc.
415 Jackson Street
San Francisco, CA 94111 USA
www.weldonowen.com

WELDON OWEN INC.

Group Publisher, Bonnier Publishing Group John Owen
President, CEO Terry Newell
Senior VP, International Sales Stuart Laurence
VP, Sales and New Business Development Amy Kaneko
VP, Publisher Roger Shaw
Executive Editor Elizabeth Dougherty
Assistant Editor Sarah Gurman
Associate Creative Director Kelly Booth
Senior Designer William Mack
Production Director Chris Hemesath
Production Manager Michelle Duggan
Color Manager Teri Bell

A WELDON OWEN PRODUCTION
© 2009 Weldon Owen Inc.

Library of Congress Control Number: 2009924574

ISBN: 978 1 74089 885 0

10 9 8 7 6 5 4 3 2
2011 2012 2013 2014

Printed by Tien Wah Press in Singapore.

People have been traveling on trains for almost two hundred years. This is much longer than they have been driving cars or flying in airplanes. The earliest trains roared along the tracks with the power of steam. Today, some of the latest high-speed trains don't even have wheels!

We use trains to take us to work, to visit family and friends, or to go on vacation. Trains also carry mail, food, and other cargo over long distances. Hop onboard to find out even more about trains.

To power a steam engine, burning coal heats water to create steam.

Some old trains run on narrow tracks. They are good at climbing steep hills.

Today, diesel fuel powers
most train engines.

An electric
train connects
to a live wire
above the line
or to a live rail
alongside the
regular track.

Streetcars, also called "trams" or "trolleys," often run on tracks buried in city streets.

Some cities have monorail trains that zoom from stop to stop. They travel along a single, or "mono," bar track that also supports the train.

Shuttle trains take people short distances, for example, between airport terminals.

Double-decker trains have two levels inside. Where would you like to sit: upstairs or downstairs?

High-speed trains go really fast. The front of the train is sleek and smooth to help it go faster.

This Japanese bullet train, called "Shinkansen," was the world's first high-speed train. Today, Japanese bullet trains carry hundreds of thousands of passengers a day.

The train yard is a busy place.
Railroad switches allow trains to
move from one track to another.

Trains travel in all kinds of weather and get dirty. These automatic washers clean them.

All aboard!
The conductor
makes sure all
the passengers
are safely on the
train. The train
and the driver
are ready to roll.

Once you're onboard, it's time to enjoy the ride. You can eat in the dining car or look out the window.

Before trains, it was impossible to travel in some mountain regions. Now, you can see amazing places on your trip!

Trains also make it easier to transport people or goods across deserts.

Trains can work in snow. The wheels of a "cog" train (below) click into notches on the tracks to prevent slipping.

Trains travel in tunnels when they can't be on the surface. Sometimes they have their own bridges.

Light-rail trains powered by electricity speed through cities. Some can run automatically and don't need a driver.

Rapid transit systems help people get around cities quickly. Some run on elevated tracks above the streets.

Subway systems run in
tunnels under city streets.

Freight trains carry heavy loads, often long distances. Some pull more than a hundred cars in a row.

Freight trains move goods, such as lumber and coal. They also move food and livestock.

Passenger trains that take people from city to city are much faster than streetcars and subway trains.

The very fast
Eurostar train
connects Great
Britain, which is
an island, to the
rest of Europe.
It goes through
a long undersea
tunnel.

You'd need your pajamas for a train ride on the Trans-Siberian Railroad. This train makes the longest journey in the world: almost 6,000 miles across Russia. The journey takes over a week!

With all of the exciting places trains can take you—where would you like to go?

Steam train

Steam trains were invented in the 19th century. They run on coal and water. Coal is burned to heat the water, which creates steam to power the engine.

Narrow-gauge railroad

Narrow-gauge railroads are frequently used in mountains because they can go around tight curves. This is the Durango-Silverton train in Colorado.

Diesel train

Rudolf Diesel patented the engine named after him in 1892. By the 1950s, diesel trains fueled by gasoline replaced steam trains and are still popular today.

Electric train

Electric trains run on electricity typically from wires above the line or from a third rail alongside the running track. They produce less pollution than diesel trains.

Streetcars

Streetcars, also called trolleys or trams, run on rails in city streets. They can be self-propelled, which means that they can go without an engine pulling them.

Monorail

Monorail trains run on just one rail. The fastest kind is the maglev, short for magnetic levitation. Running on magnets and electricity, it actually floats above the rail!

Shuttle

Also called "people movers," shuttle trains transport people short distances, for instance, between terminals at an airport. Overhead ones are called "sky" trains.

Double-decker train

Trains with two levels have more room for passengers. These trains are often used for commuter routes, where many passengers are going to and from work.

High-speed train

High-speed trains typically travel around 200 miles per hour, about three times as fast as cars travel on the highway. Japan has a lot of high-speed railroads.

Cog train

Cog trains can go up steep hills. They have wheels that click into notches on the tracks to prevent slipping. They are frequently used at ski resorts.

Subway train

Many large cities have subways, railroads that run underground. Riding the subway can sometimes be faster than driving when there's lots of traffic.

Freight train

Freight trains transport heavy cargo, such as coal. Sometimes "piggy-backed" trucks drive right onto freight cars and drive off at the end of the journey.

ACKNOWLEDGMENTS

Weldon Owen would like to thank the staff at
Toucan Books Ltd, London, for their assistance
in the production of this book: Cynthia
O'Brien, Author and Researcher, Ellen Dupont,
Project Editor; and Colin Woodman, Designer.

CREDITS

Key t=top; b=bottom; iSP=iStockphoto;
SST=Shutterstock; AL=Alamy
Jacket SST; **inside flap** SST; **2** SST; **5** SST; **6**
SST; **8**t iSP, b SST; **9** SST; **10** SST; **11**t, b SST;
12 SST; **13** SST; **14** SST; **15**t, b SST; **16**t SST,
b iSP; **17** SST; **18** SST; **20** iSP; **21**t SST, b iSP;
22t, b SST; **23** iSP; **24** SST; **25**t,b SST; **26** iSP;
28 SST; **29** SST; **30** SST; **31** SST; **32** SST; **33**t
iSP, b SST; **34**t, b SST; **35** SST; **36** SST; **37**t
SST, b SST; **38** iSP; **40** SST; **41**t SST, b SST;
42t SST, b SST; **43** SST; **44** SST; **45**t SST,
b SST; **46** SST; **48** SST; **49** SST; **50** SST; **51**t
SST, b SST; **52**t SST, b SST; **53** iSP; **54** SST; **55**t
SST, b SST; **56** AL; **58** SST; **60** SST; **64** SST.